Those Yellowed Letters

Those Yellowed Letters

Frances Skinner Reeves

palreeves@netmaxx.net

To order additional copies of this book, contact:
Xlibris Corporation
1-888-795-4274
www.Xlibris.com
Orders@Xlibris.com
81460

This book is dedicated to

Charles

who encouraged me, gave me moral support, and believed
in me. He gave me the courage to take risks. His love will
remain in my heart always.

Prologue

Why did I keep those letters? They were written 65 years ago. I had not kept other letters, much more meaningful and sentimental to me. Why had I kept those letters? Had I moved them to the few houses I had lived in during those sixty-five years? Or had they stayed stored away in my childhood home, where I have lived again for the past twenty years? Flakes of old paper fell on the floor as I looked through the scrapbooks containing prom cards, clippings of news articles about parties given or attended, and pressed corsages from dances. I found the letters stored away with other childhood and college scrapbooks and mementos. They were yellowed and tied with a rotting white ribbon. I was looking for the letters. The time had finally come for me to tell their story.

I had just entered my junior year at Mercer, having transferred from Sullins, a private girls' Junior College in Bristol, Va. It was the fall of 1945. Many veterans were returning to college after having served their country during World War Two. I was lucky to be at Mercer. (The boys outnumbered the girls four to one.) A married friend who had lived in my home area had encouraged me to attend Mercer. He was president of the student body and was a big wheel on campus. He and his wife seemed to take pleasure in introducing me around and getting me involved in campus life. His wife was in the Alpha Delta Pi sorority, which I pledged, and he was in the Alpha Tau Omega fraternity, who soon made me their Pledge Sweetheart.

To my delight, I was having a great time. Having been in a very strict girls' school during the war years where boys were really scarce, I was now experiencing the joy of being a popular girl on campus. I was having a lot of dates with boys from various fraternities and some non-fraternity boys. That is until Ed, the president of ATO, seemed to think that I was his girl. I really didn't care for Ed at all. He had returned from the war, and to me, seemed to be a bit weird. He had red hair, was lanky, and had the first contact lenses I had ever seen. It made him look like he had two glass eyes. I was not attracted to him at all. When he asked me for dates, and I had no previous engagement, I couldn't say "no", for I never wanted to hurt anyone's feelings. If anyone was ever persistent, Ed was. He would write me letters—long letters—and put them in my mailbox. The campus post office was in the Co-Op, and each student had a box, which had a combination on the front. Somehow Ed found out my combination and would put letters in my mailbox. I would get them between classes, and would just get angry at having to read them. Many times I could not understand what he was saying, but somehow I realized he had a unique style of writing. I guess that's why I kept the letters all those years. Maybe I thought he would turn out to be a great writer one day, and then I could say "Look what he wrote to me during his college days!"

All the letters he wrote me were *not* kept. But those that remain do tell a story. I've tried to guess at the chronological order in which they were written, for none of them were dated. I've not changed anything. I just copied them as they were written, including misspelled words, grammar, and punctuation. The names of the letter writer, his brothers and home town have been changed to protect their identities. Many of the letters made no sense to me; they sounded somewhat like a pre—Dr. Seuss.

The nickname I've been called all my life is "Pal". (My father's only "sons" were my sister and I, and he called us "Buddie" and "Pal".) Ed had a pet name for me—"Sparrow". Occasionally in the letters he called me "Crip", for I had sprained an ankle while wearing my galoshes, jumping a rain puddle, on campus. Now that you have the background, here are his saved letters.

LETTER ONE

(This was written on seven index cards, taped together, and
folded accordion style)

There was a little girl named Skinner
She was oh, so demure
If you didn't know what's in 'er
You'd say you really never knew 'er.

A Petunia little sparrow called Pal
With a nutty but nice roommate
Hubba, Hubba, they say she's quite a gal
'Specially in a taxi on a big big date!

But, y'know there's much more to it
Than moonlight rides and barbecue—
There's a bit of credit due it—
I mean the other things, too.

You see, there's the charm of starry eyes,
The lazy, perfect sublimity there
And in all—the ecstasy of moonstruck sighs-
Hold a touch of pure, unmitigated dare.

Certainly, the very thought of Ed
Gives you a funny feeling of positive hate
Your blood turns a ruddy red
And your fury hops like mad—on a skate!

The ends of your toes curl like orange peels
And the fire in your eyes
Burns and brims till it sorta feels
Like a bunch of charcoal pies!

Or does your funny little nose turn up
And your face get like green neon
The dimples right there just turn up
And chills down your spine—they'll be gone.

Your hair turns grey—then pink
And all the naughty gremlins and jeepers
Yaaa yaa at you whenever you think
Of the redhead who's always saying—
"where'd ya get them peepers?:"!"

Then, at night when you're fast asleep-
You dream of that awful, leering face-
Of the demon who seems determined to keep
On and on till you put him in his place.

You wonder what the Guy's got
That can possibly keep him ticking
You'd think he'd dry up and rot
'Cause he's taken so many a licking.

Then you hear him say—strongly
That he's been a bad little boy
That the world hasn't treated him wrongly
It's just that he ain't forgotten—there's still some joy!

When you see him—you always cringe
With that sharecropper walk and measly smile
The face like a horse—as if "He stays on a binge"
A beat-up frame—skinny and rough—like a file.

Maybe he'll amount to sumpin—someday
Probably got ideas and a song in his heart
I'll readily admit that all that is o.k.
But he's not got a chance—right from the start.

LETTER TWO

Well, *You* *started* this letter-writing stuff!

First off—let me rant & rave awhile about what I was talking to you last nite. Here's the score, Sparrow, We thought Jim was rather clever and a fine fellow when we first knew him. Thought he would be a great A.T.O., and he was all for it—but his Dad is a staid conservative preacher and just does not believe in fraternities.

Nathan was living in a room in our suite, and though he got along wonderfully with us and chatted with me for hours at a time in his room,—he was and is peculiarly dogmatic in his distaste for anything fraternity. Somehow—Jim was sucked in on that, and now they're like two peas in a pod.

I'll admit, we are mostly responsible for what you have come to think of Jim. But, *we* saw him for what he *ain't* and dropped him like a hot potato.

I don't care to say anything that would antagonize you, for I've got no cause to—but, I personally think he is a conceited ass—yes'm I'll grant you he may have a lot of "charm"—and I like him—but he's just about as sincere as a duck!

God only knows how and why you fell for him. A very likeable chap—when he wants to be—and I would go to bat for him—regardless.—Strange talk, huh??

Anyway—I *can't* say that I or many here have the same regard for him they had for a while. *Sure*—likely, there are folks who feel the same way about me. But *I* don't care—and he seems to go nuts about making himself known, seen, and liked. I do not go for that kind of stuff—it oozes and creeps all over me—though I don't realize it at the time—I can act just as congenial and be sincere about it with Jim as with anyone else, but at times, the thought of some things about him irks me something maddening.

Heck no, I've no idea of intimating that ATO would try to run your life! Do what you want to—you will anyway. Just *don't* keep drifting away from us like you've been doing—we need you and want you & you need us. Sparrow—A.T.O. is known as the *cleanest* frat. around—and you've not lost anything by being affiliated. Gosh, no. I'll not try to do anything that would cause you to wonder about your relationship with us. I simply like to, and do say what I think—so do you—Starry-eyes!

Just, please M'am, take it easy! For our sake and yours. I've a big load on my shoulders now. We are doing our darndest to get a fraternity house, and right now we want to pledge a dozen boys. I'm Worthy Master—the Big Wheel—*It*—I gotta work and keep the boys pulling together constantly. Y'know, these frat houses are o.k.!~ You can have big parties—and if we are first to get back in a house—that will be a big drawing-card in rushing from now on.

As for us I am personally concerned, I wouldn't walk across the street to save you from being pecked to death by little ducks—but, you are the deserving girl that my Brothers selected as their frat. Sweetheart—, and, as W.M. I am sponsoring you in the fraternity—so, please Baby, tread softly—be good. Don't be a sucker and go hog-wild for something you don't know a darn thing about! You got sense.

Mercer did the same thing for me at first I thought it was smart to hook on to something new and shiny—till the very glitter of it put my eyes out—then I woke up.

I'm mighty tired of talking all this serious stuff—it bores me eventually and I get disgusted at myself—but you seem to be in that kind of mood nowadays. Soooo—there it is—and here I go.

(You can be *certain sure* Lady that every man in A.T.O. is crazy about you—*that's* why I'm fussing.)

LETTER THREE

Something I always hated to do was apologize. Yes'm, I know it's Christian to be anxious to want to apologize. But I was too emphatically selfishly human instead of Christian—so I always hated to beg forgiveness. Yes, I am doing just that. Whether or not you accept it is left up to you. I am earnestly sincere in making this plea for forgiveness—and my conscience will be clear as a bell when I finish this letter.

The letter I wrote you was the nastiest, most distasteful piece of writing I ever kicked myself for even looking at. In the first place it was poor manners—next it was an untrue expression of my feelings. Believe me or not, I *had* an (did have) ulterior motive in doing it! That was the first time I have been consciously insincere in anything for a long long time. Sure, I'm eating humble pie, for I cannot do anything else and hold my head up and say that I'm a Man.

I completely misrepresented my own sentiments. *Why*, I'm not sure! True, Jim and I are not living in the same dormitory together now—but I never fail to go see him at least two nights a week, walk over to the fruit stand and eat donuts & drink a quart of milk. One night I bought the milk and he brought out a whole tin of fruitcake and chocolate covered nuts. We have been closer friends than anyone has to me in the fraternity. He simply has decided to not go fraternity at all—I don't blame him!

You've no idea what an experience it was to us to be together at Athens. We even planned to buy a car together to run around in at Mercer. We and Paul read the Bible and prayed together—and went in and licked four boys in the next room. Nope, Pal, I guess you're right—high-schoolish, that is me! I just wanted to see *how much* I *could* say that was bad! I couldn't *honestly* say those things about Jim. I went up to see him tonight about the B.S.U. bus—and he's still the same Jim as always—O.K!! While I was there, I jumped him about not coming over to my room much now. He said he just didn't want to get involved in any frat. Rushing. (All the others have been rushing him. I haven't, for I knew he didn't want to do it.) so he hasn't been coming around lately. I had told him long before that his and my friendship had *nothing* to do with fraternity—and he agreed. No, Pal, I did not *mean* those things I said about him in that letter. He'll readily admit that Nathan, Paul, Forrest and I are his best friends and I regard him as mine. *I've no cause to beg your forgiveness for the sake of our (yours and mine) friendship—for, what respect you had for me is gone now. I know.* I'm apologizing only *because* I think you are a Lady and I want so much to be a *Man*.

I'm glad you can't see me now Pal, 'cause you would call me a baby. First time my eyes have overflowed in———.

It's remorse—pure and simple. Just pray for me Pal, if you can find reason to even speak my name. Ask God that I might profit by the experience of having completely disillusioned a wonderful little Lady as to the plain truth of mere life—and having been brought from *MY* pedestal of egotism to a kneeling position with a face flushed from sheer remorse———by one clean blow. Ask him that I might become *something—a Man* and that I might never again be so absolutely foul, and careless, and ungentlemanly, and unchristian. I've hurt you and I know it—God help me!!

I'm awfully lonely, now. It's 1 o'clock Wednesday morning and it's raining outside. Just looking at Daddy's picture and wondering what he would have to say to me—maybe—"Son, you're still not too big to whip with a coat-hanger." I guess maybe he knows about what a fool I've been and he's frowning. Wish he could have stayed around a while longer—maybe I would have been a different boy.

When you put this letter up besides that other farce—you'll *think* some strange things—but I am at ease now—though what's supposed to be my heart is feeling right peculiar—and this is a time when I wish I were under a white cross on Saipan. I would have accomplished something *then,* wouldn't I, Pal? I'd have at least done a little something for my country—and I might have gone to heaven—then I would be looking down on other Ed Grey's—as they made people unhappy by saying and doing—and writing strange things. I would that God should paralyze my hand and not let me ever again hold a pen. I had a motive for writing that letter—but you would never believe me—and I'd find it hard to believe myself.

I know how skeptical of *anything* I say you must be by now, Pal. But, *this is crawling!* I would crawl on my hands and knees from here downtown if necessary.

I don't know what you've thought of me all along, Pal—but, I'm grateful that you tolerated my inconsistent ways and the *lack of anything* fine in me—that you gave me a chance to know you—I am truly grateful to you for that, Pal, *and I humbly ask your forgiveness* for the unnecessary, mean things I've done! Will you forgive me?? I'm *sorry* for what I have done and haven't done that should have been otherwise. I *don't know* whether or not you'll believe me—but this is my best, and that's all. I know I'm through as far as Mercer is concerned, for surely they will find me out, too—but I'll try not to give them cause for it.

We can't have a date for you by 6:30, Pal—but you can go along in the car with Miss Bates and one of the boys and his date and maybe there's one or two boys without dates coming on out a bit later—I'm pretty sure there is. (See, *all* the boys have dates, right now). You can sit at the table between two couples, and there'll be plenty of entertainment while the others are dancing—even if there are no extra boys. All the boys want you and are expecting you to go. I want you to go—but I know that means nothing—nevertheless—I want you to go.

I'm *not* a gentleman, Pal, but I am an honorable man—and as long as you have the understanding and tolerance to stick with us, I'll do my best to see that you have every rightful relationship with us that is desirable and correct.

I'm proud of my fraternity—I'm *glad* we have *you* as our Sweetheart—It *would* break my heart if you could not find the desire to keep on being our Sweetheart. When you think of the fraternity, just leave me out of the picture, for it will be an unpleasant one to you—and it shouldn't be that way.

Well, there you are, Pal, that's what's in my heart. You have it now. What you do with it is purely your own judgment. I have said all I can without becoming boring—and I'm through.

LETTER FOUR

Of Poetry—They say it's better
Than plain language—in writing a letter.
I know not that they're wrong or right,
But I'll write my poem and say goodnight.

Though not much more'n twenty,
Of Life I've seen and known-a-plenty.
There's been many a slip twixt cup and lip
Since I learned how carefully to sip.

From the bottom of my heart
Comes a wonderful song.
Not dumb, not smart—
I'm happy—all day long.

I've seen the stars in your eyes
I've seen the wind in your hair
I've heard your little white lies
I've learned there's something else there.

Every time I see You, Sparrow,
There's a perfectly normal desire
To reach out and grab You—like a fire
And kiss you—quick—like a winged arrow.

But, Shorty, I can't do that,
Cause I've got more respect for You
And I know very well—it's set down pat
That my thoughts are clear and my conscience, too.

No matter how much wrong I've done,
(Many times I've hit and run)
There's one thing definite and sure—
My heart is free and my morals are pure.

Whether or not it's good or bad
I'm saying (and I'm glad)
To do my very best to rectify,
Anything I've done to You—I'll try.

Come back to Me, Lady!!
I don't deserve this dealing from the bottom of the deck.
I've done nothing shady,
And I'm a wee bit lonely, by heck!!

I've sat in the corner long enough
There're things I could be doing
But, by gar, all this here stuff—
Marking time and cooing—!!

[

LETTER FIVE

(Note: the following four letters were written during Christmas break and were mailed to my home. The envelope had the postmark of the place mailed, the date, and the time. Each had a three-cent stamp, the letters E.R.G, Morgan Creek, Ga. in the left corner, and the address was simply *Miss Pal Skinner West Point, Georgia*)

Dated Dec. 17, 1945

Saturday night

Yayaya, thought you could get away, huh?? Wherever you go and whatever you do, Sparrow, I'll be right there. If you need a little help or even get sorta blue about something, just close your eyes and whisper—I'll be there just over your shoulder. And when you're having a wonderful time and don't have time to think about me, I'll back off in a corner and be there when you want me. I'll be counting the hours till I see you again Lady, but you can make them shorter and sweeter by talking to me a wee bit by way of the Post Office.

If you see ole Santa roaming around, or doing a figure eight or pirouette on ice skates over the Chattahoochee, just give him a little shove in this general direction, please m'am?! Don't know what that dear old gentleman is gonna do since there is practically nothing but air conditioning in the houses round these hyar parts. And don't you be flirting with him when he comes to your house, hear?!

I've seen beautiful things, sweet Sparrow, but I don't believe I ever saw anything I wanted to practically eat up like I did that night at the Sunday School banquet—or was it at the Phi Mu dance?—might have been any one of the thirteens of those dozens of other times I've seen you and those two stars you carry around where eyes should be! When you see my gaping at you, Lady, just jab me with a needle and call me dopey!

Surely you can't imagine how much oh-ing and ah-ing the boys did when they saw what you had given us the other day. Truly, Sparrow, the lovely little table would flatter anyone's mansion—especially so—when we put your picture under the top. It's right in front of the sofa, and when I call you on the 'phone, I'll be looking right into your enslaving little eyes. (By the way, I'll send your picture as soon as I can get it in the mail!) Lady, things like that that you always think of—that's why you've got us wrapped around your little finger! And the little things you do and say, and those you don't say and do—seem to suit us pretty well!

Gee gosh, Sparrow, I've kind of got used to seeing you around—expecting it every day, like to hear you on the 'phone. Gloryosky, I'm missing you, Sweet Lady!! Miss me just a wee bit?"—please! When you dare to poke your nose out the door and see all the cold and rain and mud, just think about ole grandpa Ed, loping out across the bottom toward the co-op with those beat up ole trooper boots and baggy corduroy trousers—the rain banging in wrinkled old face, and maybe making him wish sometimes that he had not forgotten how to cuss. Hallelujah! it's worse here at Morgan Creek than the Louisiana bayous. Great weather!————for ducks. Gives me too much time to think. (ah ah eh, no remarks!)

Where in the world did old man Reubensteinus' Gljjusgargusmoneioues little dog Czromlllzukjp go? Somebody told Brother lmclbksgpyz that cousin ljoiax was on his way to mnopq with a blmmunoojj, but I think Jake had the rsyuvwx of the 'yklmno, don't you agree??

Here comes Stardust on the radio. Man, what this guy can do to it—good! Nice! Mmmmmmm! But he's in the groove like apple juice and White Christmas.

I hope you have a wonderful Christmas, Beautiful.
I'm thinking of you,

-ED-

Won't you send me a picture of you Sparrow? I certainly would like to have one!

LETTER SIX

Sunday night

Sweet Sparrow,

Just now, one of the prettiest renditions of White Christmas that I've heard made me get that old feeling all over again. Made me want to see you even lots more. No fooling, Lady, it's tough—for some strange reason, since I've known you, that tune has come to mean even more to me—I do not know why, but it has! It crept over me, chilled me, warmed me. Silly, isn't it? But true. I literally, actually adore that song. When I hear it, I live in it, feel it, I want to touch it, smell it—why?!? Other people think that there are many more beautiful songs—but I like it over all them!

Then there's that song, "My Buddy." It does something to me that others would term "unpleasant," but it's not that way with me——it holds me, slaps me in the face, tears at my heart. I don't quite understand it. Because of the fact that it reminds me of someone I loved and lived with, I guess my feeling for it is such an intense hatred of it, that I like to hear it. It makes my eyes damp everytime. What's all this got to do with you?!? Well, I don't know, I just wanted to talk to you a while—O.K.??

Sometimes I wonder why the heck I spend any time on you at all. You have elastic fingers, you're nearly a foot shorter than I am, you have azure eyes and I don't like azure eyes—I like *blue* eyes! Besides that, they are like stars, and who in the world likes stars?! Honey colored hair, too, and honey is so, er, soooo-sticky—anyway, who can stand hot, crisp waffles and orange blossom honey on a winter's night?!

There's the radio——"Hour of Charm"—the chorus singing "Softly Now the Light of Day"——then me, Josh next, and Joseph all in a semi-circle around the fire. Mom's in the other room, addressing Christmas cards, Joseph is reading "Life", Josh's writing his wife at Dixie Gas., and I'm wondering what you're doing right now. Kinda cozy, wot? three long, wiry, tough ole country hicks parked around in lazy chairs. One very scholarly, knowing old gentleman—stocking up on current events; another, experienced, henpecked, "convict", and the other——red-headed——oh, well?!——!?' That Mother back there sho is a sweet one, Lassie. Can cook the best steak and bake lightest cake you ever put in your mouth. And, gloryosky she *must have something* to be able to put up with *three* yearlings at once. Imagine how it was when she had one 10 years old, one 5 and one 2. What a circus and chaos that surely must have been! We're all still living——but *good* !!

You'll be a getting' a little package 'bout time you get this letter. Better not open till Christmas, Sparrow. I'll find out whether you do or not, and if you do——Papa spank!!

If you don't have the bestest Christmas of ever, it will be somebody else's fault—not mine! 'cause I'm wishing that yours will be all the happiness of all of them combined.

> Tell you what I'll do-
> I'll see ya.

> -Ed-

LETTER SEVEN

(Postmarked Dec. 21, 1945)

Thursday
7 Pey Emm

Evenin' Beautiful,

Y'know Sparrow, I've been knowing you quite a while now, and I don't even know your Daddy's first name—or your Mother's either. Is it Joe? Nope? Well er, (once we had a fraternity brother named Hieronymous). Maybe it's Pete—surely not Jack! ? And your Mother's name is Ellen, or Francine? Grandma is Frances, no! ? Hmmmmmmmm. Okay! Where did you get Eleanor Frances?? And then tell me how the Pal and Buddie got in there—and what is Buddie's sho'-nuff name?" Mayhaps you have told me all this b 4, but I don't recall. Anyhoo, I'll go on calling you Sparrow.

Hey Lady, I saw in the paper that there is going to be a Peach Bowl game in the stadium at Mercer Jan. 1st.—2:30 p.m. and I've got tickets—50 yd. line. (Sho'nuff this time—they're colored blue and I've got them where I can see 'em!) *Want to go??* That night we can go to a big shindig or get in the hallelujah time they'll have downtown. Maybe we could go for a sleigh ride—'cept there ain't no sleigh——and there ain't no horse, and there probably won't be any snow either then. Wonderful thought tho' anyway, huh?? It did snow a little here the other day. You all had any? We all suttenly have had a large amount of rain and cold weathuh daown heah, honey-chile. It snowed a while, then rained some, then froze today—icicles every which-a-where.

While I was poking around in the living room today, I found three pieces of sheet music. Joseph had tried to get Mother to play them for him the other night, and I hadn't paid much attention. One of them was "Dream", another was "You Came along", and the other was—"*White Christmas*"! A very pretty arrangement and a beautiful design on the cover. So I kinda sneaks in, coyly-like y'know, and very gently and shyly asks Joseph if I might have that "White Christmas". He lets out a little moan and—"How 'bout that, I was gonna give you that for Christmas."—Okay, Sparrow, so I'm a heel! But save the verbs till January—and when I see you. I sure do like to see you when you're a wee bit agitated——then I can really see your dimples.

Well, well, well, well—whaddyaknow! Santa jumped the gun (eager beaver, that guy!) and brought me a scrumptious sweater yesterday—pockets, buttons and all! And "White Christmas" and a pocket-knife, and a suit—already!

Yiiiii Yiiiii, Joseph almost got my letter this morning. He would have probably kept it a long time, then sometime tomorrow, he'd have given it to me. Certainly glad he didn't wait at the P.O. box long enough!! Thank you Lady—that was a *smooooth* letter—do it often! I'll surely write you *every* little once-in-a-while.

Er, some big-shot guy will be in Macon at the City Auditorium the evening of Dec. 31st., New Year's Eve night—with his drums, orchestra, and stuff. I'd like very muchly to take the prettiest, sweetest girl in the 48!! Have a table 'n'everything. Floorshow—you know—the whole groovy business. Let me know will you Sweet, if you're planning to be in town that night. Suttenly would be mighty convenient! Can't think of the Joe's name right off. Not Alec Templeton, but name sounds kinda like that. Oh, well, I've heard of him, though!

For Christmas—lots o' folks want Cadillacs, minks and stuff,
Me, I just want to keep what I got, that's enough.
A warming little carol, maybe a sprig of mistletoe
And the sweetest little gal that God ever let me know.
Sparrow Sweet, it's in my bones
Yeah, I mean good,—like ice cream cones
I see you, I say—"That's for me".
Aye, shure and *I love you,* Lassie.

Ed

LETTER EIGHT

(Postmarked Dec. 23, 1945)

Sunday Night

Chicory, chicory, chic—waitin' by gummy for that leetle ole man with the jolly little tummy. Certainly is inconvenient, buzzin' around hyere—"Slow up", the Ego says, "or Jove! You'll fall on yer ear!"

Come next week-end, Young 'un, I'm a comin' to LaGrange! It'll probably be Saturday—Saturday afternoon—or Friday afternoon maybe. And, Lady, you better put on your courtin' shoes, 'cause I'll be 'round to get you 'bout 1 ½ minutes to 8!! If I come in the car, we'll certainly roam the banks of the Chattahoochee while I'm there! Be ready to have a big heap of fun, "cause I've got the Christmas Spirit, and I've missed you like—. O mygoodnessgraciousgloryoskyhalleluyah!! Yes'm I'll let ye know 'bout Wednesday when I'll be there—O.K.??

"Here goes nothing", I says as I start reading "Looking Backward"—by Edward Bellamy! Blimey to Geronimo, Sparrow,—I'll be a durned Socialist, yet! The guy writes about a fictitious bird who goes to sleep in his comfortable cellar, in 1887, and wakes up in 2000. He goes up to the rooftop with the owner and looks down on his native Boston. You can well imagine what a gosh-awful feeling he had in his throat when he saw what a change! Then he dazedly starts questioning this Dr. Leete about social and economic standards. Back in 1887, the man, Stan West, had been having quite a bit of unpleasantness with strikes. The people building his new house became a wee bit gripey and dissatisfied, and

West was a wealthy, impatient Gentleman—so it was worrying him no end. Incidentally, West went to sleep that night in 1887 with this trouble in mind. Pretty hard for him to comprehend when he woke up and was told he had slept 110 years! Back to my story, though. Listen, Lady, this is life what am divine and de berries, too! "Yes", said Dr. Leete, "Everybody has the same income. Industry is under one big head. Everybody is paid equally because all are of course expected to have the same *incentive,* same *sense of duty!* They are not paid for what they produce individually, but their incentive—their *will to work.*" Then it goes on telling about the idea of no one's having money to trade with. *Everybody* is issued the same individual card and it's punched when they "buy" something. *Everybody* goes to school till he's 21, then works at good, hard labor for three years—on October 15, of every year—all 24 years old retire. Oh, phooey! I'll tell you more about it later!

Let's talk about *You* for awhile. Thanks, Sparrow, for being the one and only girl I've known who I can truly say has that certain beauty and charm that makes of intelligent dignity a something that I can really latch on to and put my faith and trust in! Believe me, Sweet, I've known what good stuff you are made of since————oh, well I *know now*——that's what is important!~ Stay in the groove, Sparrow, and everybody will love you like *I* do——?

Just now, I'm a bit worried about the success of lesjjolefmolerkorodlelmgatuskye in determining the locumtoneskynovjjjiootbx on the left of the jobathumwaabbkssgi————any ideas—??

If *wishing* and *hoping* does any good, your banquet for the store was marvelously successful in every way—'cause I surely hope it was——? ! And you had enough quail for everyone? Hallelujah, Lovely, it certainly must have been a huge affair, hmnmmmmmmmmmmm! I like the very sound of it—not to mention the delicate aroma and taste of tender quail! Gloryosky, Sparrow, one or two of that kind of party and I would be *too* bubbling with exuberance 'n everything!

Our old fireball Buddy, B & G. Patton died this morning. Y'know, Sweet, *I* think—I *know*—that I firmly believe that there's good in *everybody!* Even Hitler may have been some good! I like everybody! Patton believed in God—firmly. I believe in God—that Buddy of mine who died—the "swellest", biggest hearted ole son-of-a-gun I ever knew—Yes, he *believed,* too. He died on the same soil that General Pat. died. He fought for the same wonderful things Patton died for!

After all, Sparrow, can not a man be a *man without* being a *"Saint"*?! Can't *I* be a Christian Gentleman and still *not* condemn a fellow citizen for smoking?! I do not smoke, or drink or act like a moral idiot—neither do I carry around a saintly countenance and stick my verbs with passages from the Bible. No thank you, I'll go on being Ed the rest of my life! I'll not smoke, nor cuss, nor drink, nor buzz around like a scalded monkey! I will love my God and do my best to help others love him, but I'll *not try* to be a "Saint" nor a human angel! If I like somebody (and I do like everybody) I will do something for them—with them—when I can! If I *love* somebody, I am willing to make myself one-half of a whole instead of being a selfish fool! And it will be a love that is my idea & ideal of Love—Pure, unselfish, wholesome, Holy, smiling, powerful, sweet, genteel, human, visible and invisible, tangible and intangible, infinite, carefree—It will be *Love!!* And I will fight for it, hold to it and put my heart and soul into it—the building of it, the driving and upkeep of it——*That's Me !!*

Boo! Reckon maybe you could spend a couple nights in LaGrange with Dot this weekend? Suttenly would be convenient! I surely will want to see West Point, etc., but perhaps it would be much better if you could stay with Dot some?? And I could see you a lot more that way! Or do you want to see me? I *want* to see *you* Lady, it's been a long, long time!

Papa Skinner must surely be a very tolerant, patient, loving fellow—contending with *three* such incurably curious peculiar people as he does!! The elder one has a wonderful voice, a bewitching personality and perfect beauty, the youngest—lovely hair and eyes, very neat figure, and music in her whole Self! The other one, Eleanor Frances (Palsky, for shortsky)—Oh, she's a Sad Sack—She's got *all* those things!!

What a family! Gloryosky!

I guess maybe I'm crazy 'bout all of em!!

Or is it that I know that one of them is all of them combined and I sho 'nuff Love Her?!!

Well——tell you what I'll do—

      See ya.

      -Ed-

LETTER NINE

(Back at Mercer)

Here we go again, Sparrow.

Did you have a nice weekend? I went home. Feel like a stupid fool dating these little old hometown high school girls.

First off, I want to try to straighten out this little business you cooked up last week. Now listen young 'un—think back over the whole time I've been dating you—have I ever once given you any indication that I was desperately in love with you? No m'am. Those first two letters at Christmas time had nothing of the sort in them. When you answered and asked me to drop in at W.P. and signed it "Love", I kinda figured "Well, maybe she likes me a little bit." So I answered in the same way. What on earth could have embarrassed you about that little necklace and that bunch of roses—I can't see. *Only* your folks knew about it. I thought maybe you've had time to think it over and have realized that I have not intentionally given you *any* cause to think that I'm "in love' with you. Sparrow, you let that "woman's intuition" get the best of you—you read between the lines, and you were mistaken.

Being "in love" means a two-way affair to me, Lady, and I knew you didn't care for me. Yes'm I have about ten times as much regard and respect for you as any girl I know—but this being in love is an entirely different thing. You have to have the same feeling and more before there can really be anything deep. Neither one of us had it. I couldn't afford to be in love for I've got to make good grades at school, see? What I told you that night after we had the pictures taken was the way it was—understand?

I don't know whether it was my fault or yours that there was such an unnecessary misunderstanding. What I want is——"Get that crazy, idiotic notion out of your head and let things be like they used to be. Like you said to me once—"trust me, Sparrow—I believe everything happens for the best." For the love of Mike and everybody—quit imagining so many foolish things—It's not good for anybody.

Then there's something else, Sparrow. Maybe I shouldn't tell you—but since you have decided to have nothing more to do with me at all—I am safe in telling you. No one but Forrest knows of this—and he has been so graciously tender and brotherly—though scatterbrained—! It seems that the Doctors would have me believe that this little trouble I have with my back and head will kill me someday—at no certain time—just whenever too much of that fluid gets past a little gap in my spine—I'm gone. No, Sparrow—I *want* to *live*—they cannot make me believe that I'm really a living dead-man!

I want to live and learn something, *be* something—then I can *help* someone *else!*

Sparrow, I'm so sorry I have thrown myself on *anybody!* I can't tell people about this because I don't want them to feel sorry for me, but I hate to think that I'm imposing on anybody by asking them to fool with a man that's living on borrowed time! Please forgive me, Lady for doing it to you. I found such joy in being with you, laughing with you that it hurts me to think that I was in reality being cruel to you.

I made me feel *good*—extra good when you let me come to your home—I want to have fun—and I truly enjoyed being with you and your family—things like that weekend make me want to live even more.

Though I know you don't care for me at all, and if I did love you, I would not let myself tell you—I thank God that I have the privilege of knowing you, and of loving what you stand for and what you are. If I have bored you, or been too silly at times—I am sorry, Pal. I would not want to do anything that would make you think less of me. I covet your friendship, bur not your pity. Please, please Sparrow, don't let yourself feel sorry for me. I couldn't stand that.

It's meant more to me than I can say in mere words—knowing you—being with you. I hope I've done or said something that meant something to you.

-Ed-

We play the K.A.'s in volleyball tonight at the gym—7:30. Come if you can.

(*Note: The dozen red roses he sent had a card that read, "Each rose says I love you. How can a person love someone twelve times?"*)

LETTER TEN

This is what comes of being a psychopathic-schizophrenic. *Who* was it that *I* called unpredictable?! Now I have to resort to sneaking around writing notes. Guess maybe when I build my own dog-house I am expected to stay there—and mayhaps I deserve it?

The idea that's been in my head lately, Pal, was that I was being "used." You know the old story—if something better is not to be had right at the moment—then there's ole faithful ED! That's an opinion caused by several little occurrences in the past three weeks—*and* I've been "kicked out" of M. E. P. quite often—or, wouldn't you have sat maybe ten minutes or more with ____ _____? That's what I mean, Pal. Please, if I'm wrong or right—tell me—quick. I *still* think—I know I can have a heck of a lot more fun and the right kind—with you than with any other.

The real me is the guy in the letter I wrote you Thanksgiving—but, I like to have somebody to talk to about things a little deeper sometimes. I'm the fella who likes a good poem, a song, gardenias, a sincere smile, a good chocolate malt, to ride around out in North Highlands at Christmas time and see all the wonderful lights—happy people—I know they are, and it helps a lot to make me happy. I *need* your friendship, Sparrow. We surely believe in the same basic, essential, wholesome, best things of life!

I don't *like* to hurt anybody and when I *get* hurt, it just flattens me. Yes, I know some don't care, but you do—and if you are conscious that you've been hurting me and if you did it deliberately————? !

And I am not *possessive.* I *know what the circumstances (U.S.A.) are,* and *there* it *rests!*

Soon, the pledges, *all* of them will be initiated, and your "job" as pledge sweetheart will be just non-existent. We want you to be our Fraternity Sweetheart—exchange the crescent and stars for the Maltese Cross. Here's my pin. I'd like for you to wear it as your sweetheart pin for the fraternity until another comes. No one need ever know it's mine. It will be *only* as a symbol of your loyalty to A.T.O. Please, Pal, (you're *the* sweetest, most unaffected girl I have ever known) for *their* sake don't let what opinion you surely must have of me now affect your feelings about them. I'm my own man now and the bond, the friendship the oneness and tie of love of our fraternity is a huge part of my life. Keep this pin and wear the pledge pin till the day after they are initiated, then wear this pin—the beautiful symbol of the best fraternity—the fraternity that selected you as the one to be their pledge's inspiration and their Sweetheart—forever, Sparrow. They love you, Pal, and if they know that you and I can't even be friends, what then will I be to them—surely not the Big Brother, the guiding, staying, comforting, cheering hand I could and want to be! They love you Sparrow, and—I love you.

LETTER ELEVEN

(This letter was postmarked Jan. 26, 1946, and mailed to Wet Point)

Remember one time you said I had a "style" of writing? This'll more'n
likely spoil your appetite for *styles*—but, here goes—

Of things I love
     These are a few;
But a bit of lasting dew—
A kindly word should the fresh ardor of a sickened soul so fully renew,
The fingertips of Romance might brush my weary heart, and then, come
Love, ready me quick to fling the dart.

Should the ever desiring passions in me
So discern the same in thee,
Would that I were in thy good graces, only then could we share the joy
of fond embraces.

Give my eyes clear sight
My mind Gibraltar's might
Tell me of Byron and Keats
Give me my cool clean sheets
I'll not hear of the swatting of an elephant!

The gay smell of Nature's life,
Laughter of a wee little cricket,
Two gray sparrows and a tuning fife-
The hunter heading for a thicket.

More than one love hath a man-
These are all so finite.
Their joy is but a span
But they're true—all right.

Liquid music to quicken the pulse
A bit of a poem and a briar pipe
Not to bring a tremor and convulse
But for these—so small—a love so ripe.

My Study Hour
(Courtesy Roberts Hall)
A book, a lamp, a table, a chair
My pensiveness—a vacant stare
For the life of me
I cannot see
The infinite futurity
Of putting a windshield wiper on a dog's foot!

Hear my pleading cry
We, my roommate and I
Do quite too oft' indulge
The beastly "Battle of the Bulge".
But oh, the pure insanity of the drinking of a window pane!

Here on my study desk a strewn,
The little things have no glitter.
It's but a mere bit too soon
To say my character is fitter.

Nay—there's a picture of Dad—
A preacher—with pureness of heart
A bottle of ink and a blue note pad—
Each a cog in the wheel of my life—a part.

Real, sure evidence of striving
For something real—once a dream.
Not a constantly straying diving thing
But one sure hope—a living gleam.

Here's a mirror on the wall
A snapshot of Lauren Bacall
A number card snitched from the "Pig"
My beat-up hat—way too big!

Where's the pinwheel—and the balloon?
Oh yeah, look over there, Bo-
And there was a dear little tune
"bout the Sweetheart of A.T.O.

The lingering memories of "White Christmas"
Softly played—on a piano by a tree
And the box of chocolates—all for me
Then, yes, too late to catch the bus.

LETTER TWELVE

(Note: This letter contains parts of a letter I wrote to Ed. He cut portions out, and then taped them to his answers, which follow each section. My letter is in italics. On the back of the envelope he wrote, "What a neat set of *Walking Papers* that was.!")

Ed, I've never been able to say just what I want to say, and I'm not much better at writing. But there is something I must tell you, and I believe this is the best way.

If you *had* just told me instead of writing, it would have been hard to stop me from putting my arms around you and let you talk a long time.

To put it point blank—all relationships between us must stop immediately. I'm afraid it's gone too far already, and that I should have stopped it long ago! I'm sorry it has to be this way, but it just has to be!

Yes'm that suddenness—that point blankness *did* hurt. You really cannot know *how far it* has gone until you give *it* a chance to show what *it* really is!! Yes, Sparrow, I fell—hard, but not without a long hard fight against it. I knew that maybe you have other ideas of what you want. Have you given my love a real chance? It would not have hurt a bit worse if you had let it go on till I looked into your pretty blue eyes and told you all about it——one happy night sometime. No, it has not gone too far. It had just begun. You, too, are searching for a something that's *real*. I've been looking for five years—I've found it!!—*You*. Silly prattle—you say?! I *know*, Lady—'cause I've never before had this feeling!

You have just showered me with attention, and it has gotten to the point where it is rather embarrassing. It isn't right for me to accept such and so many gifts from you. That is why I am returning the necklace. My whole family thinks I should do so, too.

Nobody but your family knew about the "gifts". (I sent the flowers 'cause I wanted to have some small part in helping you get well.) They are pulling for you and hoping you can have a very happy life. I guess maybe they don't like me much—but I like them everyone. I've been a poor country preacher's son all my life—and I've been thrown with practically *every* kind of people. I can see that your folks *know* what the score is concerning the living of the Good Life.

The little necklace was not very pretty or "elegant". I just thought you might wear it once or twice with something it would go with and then forget about it———oh, well!

It isn't fair to you, and it isn't fair to me to go along like this. It seems that I get upset more and more every time I see you. I don't know why—guess it's non-explainable. I think it is because I don't want to hurt you and yet I know it's got to be that way.

You shouldn't need to get upset. It doesn't matter too much about me. I've *nothing* to give but love. If I were *somebody*—with a great character and personality and with material wealth and a knowledge of how to use it well———it *would* make a difference—*Then,* you should not want to hurt me—but I'm *not* all that. I'm just a lean, gawky, redhead with a love for clean fun, something good to eat, nice, plain people to be with and ideas and ideals that are on a par with *any* "high classers"!

Ed, let's just have it this way—we'll say "hello" and will be sociable when we meet on campus—but that's all—no dates, no 'nuthing'.

Wouldn't that be kind of hypocritical?? I *cannot* be so casual with somebody as fine as you—I could not live with myself for long!

I hope this doesn't offend you too much, and please don't think that I am not appreciative for all the things you've done for me.

I'd appreciate it ever so much if you wouldn't even answer this note. Just give me an understanding nod when next we meet, and

No, Sweet Lady, I could *not* be offended at anything you do. A few times, I *did* get all "het up" about some little things I thought you did, but I trust you now, and figure that what you do *is* o.k. whether or not I understand it right off!

I would like very much to see you some more, but if you can't see it, I'll do my best not to miss you too much.

If you need me, Sweet Sparrow, anytime, just wink over your left shoulder—I'm right there———Loving You

-Ed-

LETTER THIRTEEN

Sparrow, 'spect I better tell you just what the score is between you and the A.T.O. You can take it as you like, but I'm not flattering—I'm speaking for the whole bunch—all 27 of us. We know you are *tops*!! We are thoroughly convinced that we scooped the campus when we got you! You have had every right and reason to drop us like a hot potato, but you have stuck!! For that we are grateful!

We pledge ourselves to love you, honor you, respect you, protect you and hold you up where the world can see you, and say, "She's ours—our Sweetheart—the girl who, come June, will wear the Maltese Cross!" And we faithfully promise to never give you cause to grieve. We want you—we believe in you and we will fight for you! If there comes a problem or a joy that we should share with you, we will. If you will do the same—Heaven can't hold a candle to the happiness we will know and enjoy. We are looking forward to the happiest, most successful years A.T.O. has ever known—and you will be right there with us!

Everybody envies us! They know that we have *the* two *choice* girls—in our Fraternity! Ask any member of any fraternity, and he will say, "Next to my own, A.T.O. is best!" It has been that way all along. Just now, we have—Student Body President, Assistant Professor of Chemistry, Assistant editor of Cauldron, Secretary of Ciceronian, Vice-president of Freshman Class, member of activities committee, 3 men in A Capella, 5 in Glee Club, 3 in Male Quartet, 2 in Blue Key, President of Blue Key, 1 Gamma Sigma Epsilon, 2 Kappa Phi Kappa, 2 Phi Beta Sigma, 3 on the Dean's list, a Summa Cum Laude graduate, 3 reporters for the Cluster, 6 or 8 high school honor graduates, 3 all-star high-school football players and rat court judge. And we are A.T.O.'s !!!!

Pat Barmore	John Hemingway
Murray Bradfield	Rufus Hodges
Marion Brantley	George Johnson
Gene Chaffine	Forrest Lanier
Guy Cheney	Joe Larkin
Fisher Craft	George McCowen
Jim Deming	Tom McLane
Bob Denney	Doyle Pratt
Roy Dunn	Tom Stewart
Ed Grey	Brad Wade
Joseph Grey	Bill Watts
Dan Evans	Ray Wilkinson
James Gray	Maurice Wynn
John Hatten	

Barmore was an A student at Dublin High—played fullback on the team there, and made Dean's list last quarter. You'd think he was nuts if you could see him come rushing into the suite at night in his pajamas, do a cartwheel on the floor and then rush out mumbling, "Well, I'll be—, forgot my pipe!" His initials are B.B.B., so we call him "Pat". Murray is constantly bustin' out with a peculiar laugh; he is "Hen".

Brantley was at Mercer, then went to Georgia some—came back here. He's known as "Mama Brantley". Chaffin is a pledge, ("Gene"), a veteran, and an honor student. Pledge Cheney ("Chink") went to N.G.C. and N.C. State and then the Navy—knows Jiu jitsu, something terrible! And adores sultry drumettes! Fisher is an alumnus, was Kappa Phi Kappa, Blue Key, Phi Eta Sigma, Gamma Sigma Epsilon and Summa cum Laude—he's "cheese-child". Jim Denning—"the Squire" is a super wolf—lurks on the Dempsey corner, clucking at cute chicks—the Coast Guard had him awhile.

Bob "Slick" Denney came from Nawth of the Mason-Dixon—He's smart and very witty—loves loud shirts & scarfs (scarves??) Roy Dunn isn't in school now, but he'll enter in March I think—came here before the army snagged him. Him—we call "Pug". Ed Grey is a Sad sack—he went to North Ga. College& N.Car. State, too and was in the army (bless 'em!). Fraternity calls me anything from "Daddy" to "Boss" to "Sleepy". Joseph "Wicked" was next to the top in High School (He and I are gonna take the track meet next spring!) and wants to be a chemist.

Dan Evans is an alumnus and has been quite a bit of help to us. James Gray is brilliant, also a judo artist and a football star (-pledge—"Bub"). John Hatten sleeps incessantly, an honor student in high school and like the name for him—"Note". John Hemingway is a pledge—very smart, army man and a good guy—he is "Genius". Rufus Hodges, a preacher's son, has the makings of a first class "Goof" and we fondly call him that—a talkative character, too. Pledge George Johnson ("Shorty") is 6 feet 4 and *smart*—very quiet boy—reserved. Forrest Lanier is a hard worker, a lovable fellow, and an expert Bull-shooter—that's "Trees" Lanier!

Joe Larkin is 40+ years old, married, has 2-3 kids and is a pledge—psychiatrist in V. Guid. Center. George "Screwy" McCowen is smart, sharp and was good in High School. Tom McLane is a dried up half-pint P-47 pilot—amiable & easygoing "Buzz boy". Doyle "Doyuuuuuulll" Pratt was Dean's list last quarter and knows a heck of a lot of mechanical things—good looking too!

Tom Stewart is a married veteran and is a prince of a fellow. Since he has such a high-pitched voice, he's "Sis". Brad Wade hails from the Chattahoochee Valley and is sometimes intelligent enough to be tagged "Brain". Bill Watts is loud but likable, went to Georgia awhile—we know him better as "Wolf, the kilowatt". Ray Wilkinson is a whiz on the piano—wears a "golden duck" and is sharp as a nigger's razor—he quickly got the name—"Hot on the 88". Maurice Wynn ("Jailbird or Shadow") is a happy guy with a huge heart and a big smile!

There you are, Shorty. The "Swellest" bunch of boys ever congregated, aggregated, or consolidated.

And we are crazy about
Our Lady from the Valley
See you, Crip

Y'know, when a man's got troubles and he looks out the window and sees a soft, golden moon and a flock of furry white clouds fooling around up there—he can't help but forget those troubles and think how lucky he is that his Mother is *not* sobbing with grief because she got a telegram from the War Department back yonder 20 months ago. I am a lucky man, Sparrow—The doctors say I'm O.K. now. I've got a future and I've got 26 fine boys to help me build it—I've got no troubles. There's beauty in a penny pencil, there's sweetness in saying "Hello", there's Loveliness in every little bug—and there's God everywhere. He's been there all the time—with his hand on my shoulder—I just couldn't feel him.

There'll be wonderful parties and fun and little heartwarming serious moments for us together, Sparrow—you and your Brothers, and we'll cherish every one!

Never have I seen a girl with so many sweethearts—27 of 'em. You must tote a battery around with you!? Or *do* you generate your own—electricity?

Epilogue

After realizing it was time to write the story of Ed, I thought perhaps I should get his permission—if he is still living. In the total 65 years since I had seen him, I had not seen him at any Mercer function nor had heard any word of him (nor had I asked).

I searched the web, with no luck. I tried the Mercer Alumni directory, with no luck. There was a link to get help from the Mercer Alumni Office. I wrote asking for any information on an Ed Grey who had been a student at Mercer during 1945. I stated that he was from Morgan Creek, Ga. and had a brother Joseph Grey who was there at the same time. I explained that I intended writing a piece that had his writings in it and wanted to get his permission to use it. Immediately I received an answer that they had a phone number for him but would have to contact him to get his permission to give his number to me. That night his number was sent to me. Fast response. A good sign!

The next day I called him. His first words after a greeting were, "'I've been wanting to apologize to you for years for the way I treated you. I'm so glad I have the chance to now. I acted so crazy, and I gave you such a hard time." I assured him that he owed me no apology, but that I perhaps owed him one. I found that he was in bad health. "They won't let me drive anymore. They say I'm too old. My wife can drive still, but she has to get around on a walker. She was in a bad wreck several years ago. I have had a heart attack and other ailments, but we're still here"

We discussed our lives since our Mercer days. He had ended up being owner and publisher of two weekly newspapers. I told him that I had always suspected that he would end up writing, for he had a real knack for it. He was now living in Augusta, Ga because his wife's work had taken them there. They had four children, two boys and two girls.His brother Joseph had also had a heart attack, and that he (Ed) had passed close to West Point while visiting him in Alabama at one time. Joseph is now living in Savannah. I told him that I wished he had stopped in to see me, and that if he were ever this way again to please come by.

He inquired about my family and situation, and seemed genuinely glad to hear from me. I told him that I had married his fraternity brother Tom McLane when Tom had graduated from Mercer Law School, and that we had four boys. I said, "You may find this hard to believe, and I don't' really know why we did it, but we named our second son 'Ed'". Ed replied, "I thought you would never even want to talk to anyone ever again by that name." I told him that after twenty-six years, Tom and I had gotten a divorce, and that I had married Charles Reeves. Both are now deceased, and I thought it was time for me to write my memoirs.

"The main purpose of my call", I said, "is that in my memoirs I want to include the letters you wrote. I am asking for your permission." His response was, "If I didn't say anything offensive, use bad language, or anything that would put me in jail, okay."

We talked on for a while about our lives for the past sixty-five years. Then as we closed the conversation, he said, "Do you really mean that I could come by to see you sometime?"

My answer? "Of course!"

About the Author

Eleanor Frances Skinner was born in Selma, Al to Thula and O.G. Skinner. As her father began opening furniture stores in Alabama and Georgia, the family moved to LaGrange, Ga when Frances was nine years old. They lived there only one year, then moved fifteen miles south to West Point, Ga, which was a more centrally located town for his growing chain of furniture stores in Georgia and South Alabama.

Frances attended Sullins Junior College in Bristol, VA. She then was graduated from Mercer University in Macon, GA with a B.A. degree, majoring in Psychology and getting minors in English, Christianity, and Education.

When her four sons were older, she went to Auburn University, obtaining a Masters Degree, a Specialist Degree, and a Doctorate in Education. She specialized in Marriage and Family Counseling, spending one summer in Sweden and Denmark studying Human Sexuality, with the University of New York.

She practiced as a therapist with a Mental Health Center in East Alabama and in LaGrange, GA. and taught many classes in Effective Parenting.

When her father was eighty years old, her sister and she decided that if they were going to inherit the business someday, they should get into it and learn from their father, who was still active in the business. They stayed there 'learning' from him until he died at ninety-five. She states, "We must not have learned well, for the business closed after his death."

Frances has served on the Mercer Board of Trustees, the Auburn Alumni Board, the Auburn Advisory Board of Human Relations, and The Auburn College of Education Advisory Council. In 1992 she was one of 400 women honored as outstanding Auburn Women Graduates in Celebration of the Centennial of the Admission of Women to Auburn.

Always active in Christian endeavors, since her retirement in 2000 Frances has continued to be active in church, community, civic, and educational affairs. In 2008 she was encouraged to participate in the Ms. South West Georgia Senior pageant where she won the title. She firmly believes that even though one is older in years, she can still be active and have fun.

This book is her first published endeavor.